To:-
From:-

OTHER BOOKS IN THE TO-GIVE-AND-TO-KEEP® SERIES:

Welcome to the New Baby	To a very special Dad
To a very special Daughter	To a very special Friend
Merry Christmas	To a very special Granddaughter
To a very special Grandpa	Wishing you Happiness
Happy Anniversary	To a very special Husband
To my very special Love	To a very special Grandmother
To a very special Mother	To a very special Son
To my very special Wife	To a very special Teacher
To a very special Grandson	To a special Couple on your Wedding Day

Published simultaneously in 1994 by Exley Publications Ltd. in Great
Britain, and Exley Giftbooks in the USA.

12 11 10 9 8 7 6 5 4

ISBN 1-86187-362-X

Copyright © Helen Exley 1993
The moral right of the author has been asserted.

Edited by Helen Exley.
Printed in China.

Exley Publications Ltd, 16 Chalk Hill, Watford, Herts WD19 4BG, UK.
Exley Publications LLC, 185 Main Street, Spencer, MA 01562, USA.
www.helenexleygiftbooks.com

'TO A VERY SPECIAL'® AND 'TO-GIVE-AND-TO-KEEP'®
ARE REGISTERED TRADE MARKS OF EXLEY PUBLICATIONS LTD
AND EXLEY PUBLICATIONS LLC.

To *a very special*®
SISTER

WRITTEN BY PAM BROWN
ILLUSTRATIONS BY JULIETTE CLARKE

However distant we are from
one another, however life has
changed us, we are linked forever.
You will always be a very special
part of my life.

A HELEN EXLEY GIFTBOOK

▨EXLEY

A SISTER IS...

Someone to tell my secrets.

Someone to share my adventures.

Someone to show my acquisitions.

Someone to stick up for me.

Someone to take care of.

Someone who will be there in times of fear or

sickness and in times of joy.

Someone just like you.

. . .

A sister is someone to experiment on, someone to comfort, someone to scold.

A sister borrows just about everything you possess – and sometimes gives things back.

A sister tells on you to your parents.

A sister accidentally lets out secrets.

A sister gets away with things you don't or never could.

A sister turns to you when she's in trouble.

A sister nags, tells you to comb your hair, ties up your shoelaces.

A sister says she's too busy to help you with your homework.

A sister moans when she has to take you for a walk.

A sister puts you to bed when you've got 'flu.

A sister punches bullies who attack you.

A sister loves you. Most of the time.

Everyone needs a sister.

. . .

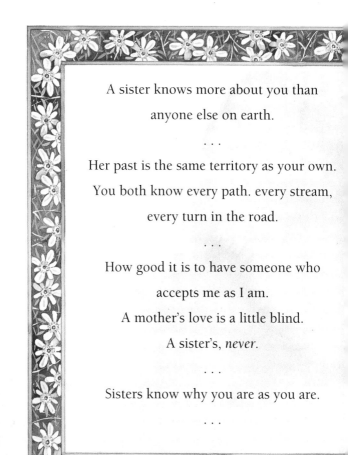

A sister knows more about you than
anyone else on earth.

. . .

Her past is the same territory as your own.
You both know every path. every stream,
every turn in the road.

. . .

How good it is to have someone who
accepts me as I am.
A mother's love is a little blind.
A sister's, *never*.

. . .

Sisters know why you are as you are.

. . .

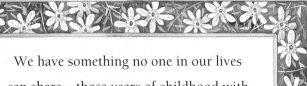

We have something no one in our lives
can share – those years of childhood with
their hopes and terrors, their secrets
and their plans.
Only we know what made us as we are
today. Only we remember the small
victories and sorrows for we know the
whys and wherefores.
We know each other's hearts.

. . .

Friends get the slightly expurgated
version of your life.
Sisters know the original text.

. . .

EVERYONE SHOULD HAVE ONE!

If you haven't got a sister, you've a hole
in your life.

. . .

My second mum, my first friend –
that's my sister.

. . .

There's Mother's Day and Father's Day.
– There should be a Sister's Day –
especially for you.

. . .

Everyone needs a sister

to advise on insurance and electrical appliances and

perennials and the right sort of lawn seed.

On spanners and steam irons.

On cars.

Everyone needs sisters

to give them foolproof recipes and the best

route to Birmingham.

To exchange mortgage information.

To listen.

. . .

DO YOU REMEMBER?

Do you remember whisperings in the dark, the
secrets, the schemes, the gigglings? And quiet tears.
Paddings from bed to bed. Do you remember
Christmas mornings? – "I've got a *doll*,
I've got a *bear*, I've got an *harmonica*."
Do you remember padding about the kitchen in the
dawn-light, getting Dad's birthday breakfast?

The hushing and the clattering and the smell of
burning toast. Do you remember sharing the bath?
– the bubbles and the splashings and the wailing
when the soap got in your eyes? Do you remember
falling into the stream? The scoldings lost in
laughter? And the mud.

Do you remember Saturday morning dance class?

Do you remember when the cat had seven kittens?

Do you remember getting lost? And found?

Do you remember the scrunching of

forbidden sweets?

We are grown and very different now. People say –

"I would *never* have taken her for your sister."

But we share the glimmering dark, birthday cuddles

among Mother's pillows – and the safety

of Dad's arms.

We share a secret land where no one else can come.

For we are bound together by a thousand memories.

. . .

After the party, when the dishes have been washed

and the worst of the mess cleared away ("we'll leave

the rest till morning"), sisters sprawl in their chairs

and sleepily begin the game of

"Do you remember.....?"

. . .

<u>MORE THAN A FRIEND</u>

Friends we can discard.

Sisters are with us forever.

And so we learn to accept each

other as we are.

Good and bad.

Which is a most comforting feeling.

. . .

You never really know your friends –

you made their acquaintance

too late in life.

Sisters you *know*.

. . .

Your partner is fine.

But for the nitty gritty family stuff,

one needs a sister.

Like you.

. . .

When friends are not enough – I'm glad I have your telephone number.

. . .

Friends find each other. Siblings are there from the beginning – no choice involved.

We know each other inside out, upside down, bad and good, with no acted roles, no disguises and no secrets.

And so we like each other, love each other, need each other, in a different way to friends. For we're so interlocked with part of one another.

We've differed sometimes, and squabbled,

And a hint of sibling rivalry will haunt us even when we are very old.

But the link is there forever.

You know who I really am – and accept me. And forgive me. And are concerned for me.

The way I am for you.

. . .

TROUBLED TIMES

Sometimes you just need a hand to hold – and
sisters know when.

. . .

You can turn up on a sister's doorstep at any
time and in any state and be sure of a cup of
tea and a listening ear....
And a bed if it's *really* bad.

. . .

Who would I turn to i
a dire emergency
but you?

. . .

When the sky falls in, a sister will
lend you an umbrella.

. . .

When something wonderful happens, first you
phone your partner, then your mother
– and then your sister.
When something appalling happens
– you phone your sister.

. . .

Sisters *know* why you are in the mess you're in.

. . .

Often siblings don't see much of each other once
they've grown and gone – nor do they write or
telephone. But their lives are inextricably entwined
and distance cannot dim their mutual concern.
When trouble comes all sibling rivalry is forgotten
and they give all their energies to comfort,
aid and rescue.

. . .

A VERY SPECIAL ...

No one thanks sisters or praises sisters or writes songs about them. Sisters are simply there – like your right arm. They are totally themselves – but somehow a part, too, of your own life. They flounder in and out of your existence. They know too much about your past. They have memories like elephants. They know your weak spots. They are inclined to sigh and say: "Well – you *would*, wouldn't you?"

But when you are stuck at a bus station in the mountains, or on a country road, when the river has changed course and is running through the living room, when you have bumped the car rather badly, when your partner has just left for good, when you've *all* gone down with the flu, when you have a nasty and persistent pain... sisters are simply there.

. . .

THE BEST AUDIENCE

Who greets the news of your most incredible
achievement with, "*Good.* I *told* you that you
could do it?"

. . .

You are the person I can't wait to tell good
news, a joke,
an adventure,
an astonishment.
It's only when I hear you gasp, hear you
giggle, hear you laugh out loud – only
when I see your eyes grow wide –
that the joy's complete.

. . .

Sisters are different. They heard
the sobbing in the darkness.
They lived through all your triumphs,
all your failures, all your loves and losses.
They have no delusions. They lived with
you too long.
And so, when you achieve some victory,
friends are delighted – but sisters hold your
hands in silence and shine with happiness.
For they know the cost.

. . .

Sisters stand beside you in your hour of
triumph and catch your eye and grin.
They are glad for you
– but never dazzled.

CHIEF DEFENDER

Sisters annoy, interfere, criticize.

Indulge in monumental sulks, in huffs,

in snide remarks. Borrow. Break.

Monopolize the bathroom.

Are always underfoot.

But sisters are your second self. And if catastrophe

should strike, sisters are there. Defending you

against all comers.

. . .

Every small child needs a sister to leap
to their defence.
A brother will do – but sisters are more ferocious.

. . .

"I'll tell my SISTER" seemed a pretty silly warning to
bullies – until they called my bluff.

. . .

Sisters live their own separate lives, phone
on occasion, remember birthdays. It seems
so casual. But let disaster strike – and sisters
come roaring to the rescue.
Heaven help the so-and-so who's caused the misery!
Better to face a charging bull than a sister
on the attack.

. . .

When sisters stand shoulder to shoulder,
who stands a chance against them?

. . .

MAY

21

22

23

MISSING YOU

A sister is *there* – whatever the distance between.

. . .

Your writing on the envelope, your voice on the
phone – and at once I am alert: "What's happened?
What has she done? Where is she going?"

. . .

Brothers and sisters are never quite alone –
so long as there's a telephone.

. . .

You are just as much my sister as when we
crouched under the table together, making endless
cups of tea for our teddy bears.
I think of you so often.
Think of me a little. And *phone*.

. . .

Thank you for being there. Even if I scarcely ever
see you. How lonely a place the world must be
sometimes for people who have no sisters.

Thank you for hugging me when all the
world went wrong.
Thank you for reading to me when I had measles.
Thank you for blowing my nose when I
was very small.
Thank you for holding my hand when I
was horribly afraid.
Thank you for taking care of me.

. . .

Thank you for being the sort of sister everyone
should have – a companion in adventure, a sharer
of secrets, a lender of haircombs and sweaters and
emergency money.
A friend always.

. . .

Thank you for all the last minute repairs – the
standing-up stitchings, the safety-pin anchorings,
the painted-over shoe scuffs,
the nail varnish ladder stops.
Little did they know that one good sneeze
would have me in ruins.

. . .

Thank you for all the things you've lent me. Thank
you for all the things you've sent me, made for me,
shown me how to do. Thank you for all the rescues,
all the cover-ups, all the scoldings and comfortings.
Thank you for all the laughs, all the
shared adventures.
Thank you for being there for me whenever I
needed you.

. . .

Thank you for always being there – entirely yourself
and yet a part of me.

. . .

BONDED

We have our own lives and in some ways are
so very different – but some things we share
– influences. ancestors, experiences, family
jokes, family habits, memories of grief
and joy, secrets. We understand each other
a little too well. We are inclined at times to smile
or sigh and say, "Only *she* could do
a thing like that."
We are linked together by light, invisible chains –
stronger than steel and indestructible.

. . .

Until the ending of our days, we
will be part of one another's lives.
However far apart, however
different, we are essential to
each other.

. . .

We share recollections that no one else can know.

We share sorrows that none can understand.

We share joys that are our secret treasure.

Our lives are bound together.

. . .

A sister is always our spiritual Siamese twin....

we are bonded together forever, however

separate our outward lives.

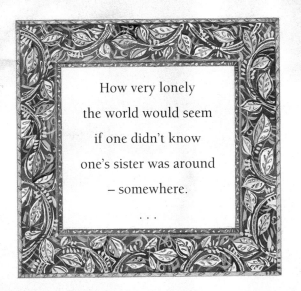

How very lonely
the world would seem
if one didn't know
one's sister was around
– somewhere.

. . .